Contents

It's autumn!

In autumn the leaves on many trees turn red and orange and brown.

Days out in

Autumn

Heinemann
LIBRARY

Little Nippers

H **www.heinemann.co.uk/library**
Visit our website to find out more information about **Heinemann Library** books.

To order:
☎ Phone 44 (0) 1865 888066
▤ Send a fax to 44 (0) 1865 314091
▢ Visit the Heinemann Bookshop at www.heinemann.co.uk/library to browse our catalogue and order online.

First published in Great Britain by Heinemann Library, Halley Court, Jordan Hill, Oxford OX2 8EJ, part of Harcourt Education.
Heinemann is a registered trademark of Harcourt Education Ltd.

Editorial: Jilly Attwood and Claire Throp
Design: Jo Hinton-Malivoire and bigtop, Bicester, UK
Models made by: Jo Brooker
Picture Research: Rosie Garai, Sally Smith and Debra Weatherley
Production: Séverine Ribierre

Originated by Dot Gradations
Printed and bound in China by South China Printing Company

ISBN 978 0 431 17303 0 (hardback)
08 07 06 05 04
10 9 8 7 6 5 4 3 2 1

ISBN 978 0 431 17308 5 (paperback)
08 07
10 9 8 7 6 5 4 3

British Library Cataloguing in Publication Data
Parker, Vic
Days out in autumn
508.2
A full catalogue record for this book is available from the British Library.

Acknowledgements
The publisher would like to thank the following for permission to reproduce photographs: Alamy/Leslie Garland Picture Library p. **10–11**; Collections p. **18** (Nigel Hawkins); Corbis pp. **17 top**, 17 bottom, **15**, **19**; Gareth Boden pp. **20**, **21**; Getty Images p. **22–23** (Pauline Cutler); Reflections p. **12** (Jennie Woodcock); Robert Harding Picture Library p. **4** (Andy Williams), **16** (Jeremy Bright), p. **6**; Robert Harding p. **14** (N. Penny); Trevor Clifford pp. **5**, **7**, **8**, **9**, **13**.

Cover photograph reproduced with permission of Alamy/John Foxx.

The publishers would like to thank Annie Davy for her assistance in the preparation of this book.

Days out in
Autumn

Vic Parker

Heinemann
LIBRARY

Little Nippers

H **www.heinemann.co.uk/library**
Visit our website to find out more information about **Heinemann Library** books.

To order:
☎ Phone 44 (0) 1865 888066
▤ Send a fax to 44 (0) 1865 314091
▢ Visit the Heinemann Bookshop at www.heinemann.co.uk/library to browse our
catalogue and order online.

First published in Great Britain by Heinemann
Library, Halley Court, Jordan Hill, Oxford
OX2 8EJ, part of Harcourt Education.
Heinemann is a registered trademark of Harcourt
Education Ltd.

Editorial: Jilly Attwood and Claire Throp
Design: Jo Hinton-Malivoire and bigtop,
Bicester, UK
Models made by: Jo Brooker
Picture Research: Rosie Garai, Sally Smith and
Debra Weatherley
Production: Séverine Ribierre

Originated by Dot Gradations
Printed and bound in China by South China
Printing Company

ISBN 978 0 431 17303 0 (hardback)
08 07 06 05 04
10 9 8 7 6 5 4 3 2 1

ISBN 978 0 431 17308 5 (paperback)
08 07
10 9 8 7 6 5 4 3

British Library Cataloguing in Publication Data
Parker, Vic
Days out in autumn
508.2
A full catalogue record for this book is available
from the British Library.

Acknowledgements
The publisher would like to thank the following
for permission to reproduce photographs:
Alamy/Leslie Garland Picture Library p. **10–11**;
Collections p. **18** (Nigel Hawkins); Corbis pp. **17
top**, 17 bottom, **15**, **19**; Gareth Boden pp. **20**, **21**;
Getty Images p. **22–23** (Pauline Cutler);
Reflections p. **12** (Jennie Woodcock); Robert
Harding Picture Library p. **4** (Andy Williams), **16**
(Jeremy Bright), p. **6**; Robert Harding p. **14** (N.
Penny); Trevor Clifford pp. **5**, **7**, **8**, **9**, **13**.

Cover photograph reproduced with permission of
Alamy/John Foxx.

The publishers would like to thank Annie Davy
for her assistance in the preparation of this book.

Every effort has been made to contact copyright
holders of any material reproduced in this book.
Any omissions will be rectified in subsequent
printings if notice is given to the publishers.

The paper used to print this book comes from
sustainable resources.

Brrr! Autumn is chilly.

What should you wear to go out?

I spy in the park

In the park the leaves make a colourful carpet.

6

What else has fallen
from the trees?

Autumn art

You can make bright autumn pictures with leafprints.

Finished!

Let's go fly a kite

Autumn winds are good for flying kites.

What shapes can you see in the sky?

Blackberrying trip

Let's pick ripe blackberries from the hedgerow.

Mmm!

Blackberry pie for pudding! Yum!

It's Halloween!

It's fun to dress up in **scary**, spooky costumes for a Halloween party.

15

Beachcombing

Cold days on the beach are good for treasure hunts.

Can you find smooth pebbles or a pretty shell?

At the fun park

choo!
choo!

At a fun park, there are lots of exciting rides to try.

giddy up!

Helping in the garden

It's time to plant bulbs in the garden.

They will grow into spring flowers.

There is lots of tidying up to do too!

fizz!

Index

The end

Notes for adults

The *Days out in...* series helps young children become familiar with the way their environment changes through the year. The books explore the natural world in each season and how this affects community life and social activities. Used together, the books will enable discussion about similarities and differences between the seasons, how the natural world follows a cyclical pattern, and how different people mark special dates in the year. The following Early Learning Goals are relevant to this series:

Knowledge and understanding of the world

Early learning goals for exploration and investigation
• look closely at similarities, differences, patterns and change.

Early learning goals for sense of time
• observe changes in the environment, for example through the seasons.

Early learning goals for cultures and beliefs
• begin to know about their own cultures and beliefs and those of other people.

This book introduces the reader to the season of autumn. It will encourage young children to think about autumn weather, wildlife and landscape; activities they can enjoy in autumn; and what clothes it is appropriate to wear. The book will help children extend their vocabulary, as they will hear new words such as *hedgerow* and *bulb*. You may like to introduce and explain other new words yourself, such as *wheelbarrow* and *sparkler*.

Additional information about the seasons

Not all places in the world have four seasons. Climate is affected by two factors: 1) how near a place is to the Equator (hence how much heat it receives from the Sun), 2) how high a place is (mountains are cooler than nearby lowlands). This is why some parts of the world have just two seasons, such as the hot wet season and the hot dry season across much of India. Other parts of the world have just one season, such as the year-long heat of the Sahara desert or the year-long cold of the North Pole.

Follow-up activities
• Make a collection of things you might find on an autumn beach walk: a feather, a bit of driftwood, a smooth pebble, a pretty shell, etc.
• Take a trip to a library to find out more about Halloween and the autumn festivals of other cultures.
• Make a pumpkin lantern for Halloween.

24

This is a Bright Sparks Book
First published in 2001

Bright Sparks
Queen Street House
4 Queen Street
Bath BA1 1HE, UK

This book was created by
small world creations ltd
25a Long Street, Tetbury, GL8 8AA, UK

Written by Ronne Randall
Illustrated by Frank Endersby

Copyright © Parragon 2001

ISBN 1-84250-245-X

This Book Belongs To:

Mrs. Simpson. (200X)

Fred the Frazzled Fireman

Bright ☆ Sparks

Fred Fireman hurried to the fire station. It was his turn to cook lunch for the firemen on his shift, and he had just bought some nice, plump sausages at the butcher's.

At the fire station, Fred bumped into Builder Benny, who had come to repair a broken window frame.

"Ooops! Hello, Benny!" he said.

Then he went straight to the kitchen to start cooking.

The smell of sausages wafted through the fire station.

"**Mmm**, those sausages smell good!" said Dan and Mike,
the other firemen, as they arrived for work.

Suddenly the alarm bell rang -

CLANG! CLANG! CLANG!

"Emergency!" cried Fireman Mike. He and Fireman Dan
rushed down the pole and into their fire-fighting gear.

"What about the sausages?" cried Fireman Fred.

"Don't worry about a thing," said Builder Benny, coming in through the window. "I'll look after them till you get back."

"Thanks, Benny!" said Fireman Fred, trying to get his apron off as he rushed down to join the others.

The emergency
was in Tony's Pizza Parlour
 - one of the ovens had caught fire!
"We'll have that blaze out in a jiffy!" said Fred, rushing in
with a big fire extinguisher. Dan and Mike followed with the hose.

With a WHISH! and a WHOOSH! from Fred,
and a SPLISH! and a SPLOOSH! from Mike and Dan,
the fire was soon out.

Tony's
Pizza
Parlour

"WHOOPS! cried Fireman Fred, slipping on the wet floor.

But he was back on his feet in a flash.

"Thank you!" said Tony, as the firemen took their equipment back to the truck.

"I can get back to baking pizzas now!"

Tony's Pizza Parlour

Just when they were ready to go
back to the station, the firemen heard a
call coming through over their radio.

"Emergency! Emergency!
Window cleaner in distress on Pine
Avenue. Emergency! Over."

"We're on our way!" said Fireman Fred, starting the engine.
"Over and out!"

NEE-NAW! NEE-NAW!

With sirens blaring, the fire engine zoomed into Pine Avenue. A crowd had gathered around Tip-Top Towers, the tallest building in town.

"It's Will the window cleaner!" cried Postlady Polly, who had just finished delivering the day's post to the building.

"His ladder has broken, and he's hurt his leg. Now he's stuck, and he can't get down! Can you help him?"

Pine Avenue

"Certainly!" said Fireman Fred. "I'll be up there in a jiffy!"

The firemen put up their tallest ladder. While Mike and Dan held out a net - just in case - Fred fearlessly began scrambling up the ladder.

"Here I come, Will!"
he shouted.

"I've got you, Will!" said Fred, grabbing hold of the window cleaner. As the crowd below cheered, Fred carried Will down the ladder and helped him into the fire engine.

Fred drove the fire engine straight to the hospital.
"Thank you for rescuing me," Will said to Fred.

"Don't mention it," said Fred. "I'm sure your leg will be fine -
but I think you'll need a new ladder!"

"What a busy day it's been!"
said Fireman Fred, as they drove
back to the fire station.
"I feel really frazzled!"

"Our work's not over yet!" said Fireman Dan.
"Look! There's smoke up ahead!

NEE-NAW! NEE-NAW! went the siren.

VRROOOM! VRROOOM! went the engine,
as it raced to the scene of the fire.

The smoke was coming from the fire station! Dan and Mike unwound the hose, and Fred raced inside. "Oof!" he gasped, as he tripped over the hose and bumped into Benny - again!

"Sorry, fellows," said a red-faced Builder Benny.
"I guess I burnt the sausages. I think your lunch is ruined."

Poor Fred felt really frazzled now - until he had an idea.

"I know just the person to rescue us from this situation!" he said.
"Who?" asked the others.

"Tony!" said Fireman Fred.
"His pizzas are yummy, and an extra-large one
will be a perfect lunch for all of us!"